7/5/21

SO YOU'RE

80!

Mike Haskins & Clive Whichelow

Illustrations by Ian Baker

summersdale

SO YOU'RE 80!

First published in 2010
Reprinted 2011
This edition copyright © Mike Haskins and Clive Whichelow, 2013

Illustrations by Ian Baker

Summersdale Publishers Ltd
46 West Street
Chichester
West Sussex
PO19 1RP
UK

www.summersdale.com

Printed and bound in China

ISBN: 978-1-84953-441-3

Substantial discounts on bulk quantities of Summersdale books are available to corporations, professional associations and other organisations. For details contact Nicky Douglas by telephone: +44 (0) 1243 756902, fax: +44 (0) 1243 786300 or email: nicky@summersdale.com.

To...............................

From..........................

INTRODUCTION

Wow! Gosh! No, never! You, 80? You can't be! Well I suppose you must be or you wouldn't be reading this book, would you?

At one time 80 was quite old, but not any more. No, 80 is the new 70. Unlike Greece, you still have all your marbles; you may even still be playing marbles. You enjoy life to the full, though you may have begun to cut back a bit on the wilder side of things.

These days, your idea of an extreme sport might be getting the top off a ketchup bottle or simply standing up straight after a prolonged session in a comfy chair, although it comes to us all eventually.

But, hey, reaching 80 is something to celebrate! So pop open a bottle of something fizzy, throw away all those preconceived ideas about what 80-year-olds should be like and have a whale of a time! You're just 20 for the fourth time round!

THE
AMAZING
OCTO-
FLEXIES
★ ★

REASONS TO BE CHEERFUL

*People will comment
on how marvellous you are,
even if you've simply walked
to the corner shop unaided*

You could join
The Rolling Stones
and not look out
of place

WHY 80 REALLY ISN'T THAT OLD

You're just a nipper compared to some of those characters in the Bible (Methuselah – 969, Noah – 950, Adam – 930, Deborah – 130, etc.)

It is said that the oldest turtle lived to be 250 – in turtle years you're not even middle-aged!

WHY 80 *IS* THAT OLD

If you were a car you'd have been crushed years ago

*The glare from your
birthday candles can
be seen from space*

*If you were a house,
you'd be in need of extensive
modernisation and new
plumbing (which, ironically,
you feel you require anyway)*

GIVEAWAYS THAT WILL TELL PEOPLE YOU ARE OVER 80

*Your house has more
support rails than a funfair
full of white-knuckle rides*

*Very few people seem willing
to accept a lift when they
find out you're driving*

WHY IT'S GREAT
TO BE 80

You can refer to almost anyone as being 'wet behind the ears' and/or a 'whippersnapper'

You can be as rude as you like and people will just think you're 'a bit of a character'

NEW MEASURES
OF SUCCESS FOR
80-YEAR-OLDS

Managing to get a whole hour's sleep between nocturnal trips to the loo

Remembering where you parked your mobility scooter

Eating a toffee without gluing your dentures together for the rest of the day

NOW
YOU'RE 80
THE FOLLOWING
WILL BE YOUR
NATURAL
ENEMIES

Any technological device introduced since the 1970s

Small print

Small print
warning of stairs

Stairs

THINGS YOU ARE NOW LIKELY TO HAVE IN YOUR HOME

A seven-day organiser box for all your pills

Tartan rugs to keep your legs warm

At least one room that looks like a small museum of antique china

YOUTH ENHANCERS TO AVOID

Plastic surgery – at your age you would probably have to have Bakelite surgery instead

*Botox – being forgetful
is bad enough, but having a
permanently blank expression
will only make it worse*

HOW TO BE PHILOSOPHICAL ABOUT BEING 80

You're still only in double digits!

You may now be entering a state of great spiritual enlightenment… alternatively it might be that you've just nodded off for a moment

George Burns had just re-launched himself as a movie star at 80, Matisse was still painting at 84 and Coco Chanel was still running her fashion empire at 85

THINGS THAT WILL REALLY MAKE YOU FEEL OLD

Meeting some doddery old
fool in the pension queue
and learning that they're
younger than you

Seeing a photograph of the rest of the family gathered round some ancient individual and then realising that it's you

*Discovering that your life
spans the entire history
syllabus being taught
at a local school*

PHRASES YOU'LL FIND CREEPING INTO YOUR VOCABULARY

'Speak up a bit
will you?'

'I'm 80 you know!'

*'Can you get this thing
to work for me?'*

'Do I know you?'

WORDS OF WISDOM YOU CAN NOW SHARE WITH YOUR JUNIORS

'My first wage packet was £1 for a 48-hour week and it was still enough to buy myself my first car and have change left over'

'Sex is a vastly overrated pastime'

HOBBIES YOU PROBABLY SHOULDN'T CONSIDER TAKING UP

Speed dating (maybe slightly-slower-than-average dating instead)

Any sport with the word 'extreme' in front of it – e.g. Extreme Tiddlywinks

Marathon running –
it's exhausting enough
just walking up the stairs
these days

WAYS FOR 80-YEAR-OLDS TO SURPRISE FRIENDS AND FAMILY

Announce your plan to do a sponsored parachute jump

Announce you're marrying someone 60 years your junior who you've just met on match.com

THINGS YOU CAN DO THAT YOUNGSTERS CAN'T

*Have a polite
conversation with a
total stranger*

Get all the drugs you need without breaking the law

Spell

PRODUCTS YOU'D LIKE TO SEE

A walking stick with a cattle prod attachment to help clear your way through the crowds at the supermarket

*Bionic replacement
body parts available
on prescription*

Additional memory –
well, if they can do it
for computers…

A walking frame with a built-in toilet in case there isn't one around while you're out

GAMES FOR WICKED 80-YEAR-OLDS TO PLAY

Guess Who's Not
In My Will?

Lying very still until people look worried then jumping up and shouting, 'Boo!'

*Pretending to be
deaf so you don't have to
respond to silly comments
from anyone*

Trapping visitors with endless cups of tea until they have listened to your entire life story

NEW YEAR'S RESOLUTIONS YOU MAY NOW ACTUALLY STICK TO

To stop gallivanting with members of the opposite sex – especially those frisky young 70-year-olds

To cut down on all-night drinking binges – unless it's Horlicks

THE UPSIDE
OF BEING 80

By now you must surely qualify as a design classic

You have survived all the things that people always said weren't good for you, such as drinking, smoking and eating food that is two days past its sell-by date

If you're interested in finding out more about our books, find us on Facebook at Summersdale Publishers and follow us on Twitter at @Summersdale.

www.summersdale.com